BRITISH PADDLE STEAMERS

The Heyday of Excursions and Day Trips

BRITISH PADDLE STEAMERS

The Heyday of Excursions and Day Trips

JOHN MEGORAN

AMBERLEY

Frontispiece: *Embassy* (1911–1967, previously *Duchess of Norfolk*) on a cruise from Swanage in June 1961.

Front Cover Top: *Queen of the South* (1931–1968, previously *Jeanie Deans*) and *Queen of the Channel* (1949–1984) near Tower Bridge, July 1966.

Front Cover Bottom: *Princess Elizabeth* (1927–present) in 1962.

Back Cover: *Consul*, previously *Duke of Devonshire* (1896–1968), alongside at Weymouth, August 1961.

First published 2016

Amberley Publishing
The Hill, Stroud
Gloucestershire, GL5 4EP

www.amberley-books.com

British Library Cataloguing in Publication Data.
A catalogue record for this book is available from the British Library.

ISBN 978 1 4456 5389 1 (print)
ISBN 978 1 4456 5390 7 (ebook)

Typeset in 10pt on 12pt Sabon.
Typesetting and Origination by Amberley Publishing.
Printed in the UK.

Contents

Chapter 1

Development of Excursion Paddle Steamers

In their earliest days at the beginning of the nineteenth century, paddle steamers were used primarily as transport and, to a much lesser extent, for excursions for the well-off.

The 1871 Bank Holidays Act introduced the idea of paid holidays for all. The expansion of the railways opened up the opportunity to travel long distances at speed, and the two together spawned the day out or holiday at the seaside, with the possibility of a trip on the briny for all.

Excursions took off from just about everywhere with a harbour or newly built pier and from beaches anywhere around the UK coast. The increasingly booming trade concentrated in several key honeypot areas, including the Clyde, the North Wales and Lancashire coasts, the Bristol Channel, the south coast and the Thames, where features of natural beauty and interest encouraged tourism, while an industrial hinterland or population centre, within easy reach in a day on the train, provided the volume of trippers to fill the boats.

At their peak, from the 1890s through to the First World War, so prolific were excursion paddle steamers that you could have boarded one at Great Yarmouth and, with an assiduous study of the timetables and connections, kept changing onto others sailing up to London, down to Kent, on along the south coast through Folkestone, Brighton, Bournemouth, Weymouth, Torquay, Plymouth and Penzance, with cross-Channel hops to France or the Channel Islands along the way, and then on up the Bristol Channel via Ilfracombe to Bristol or along the Welsh coast to Swansea, Tenby and Caldy Island.

Early excursion paddle steamers like the *Premier* (1846–1937) had a main deck with passenger saloons below forward and aft of the machinery, and a raised platform above, from which the captain conned the vessel. The *Premier* was built for service on the Clyde, and is seen here in a later incarnation in Lulworth Cove.

Many harbour and salvage tugs also had passenger certificates, and consequently enjoyed a profitable side line in offering short trips to sea from ports all around the UK when there wasn't enough towage work about. These included the *Albert Victor* (1883–1928), pictured left, *Queen* (1883–1923), pictured right, with the *Empress* (1878–1955) in the foreground at Weymouth.

The single-decked steamers gradually got bigger, like *Victoria* (1884–1952) of Weymouth, but still offered scant covered accommodation if the weather was inclement.

For longer trips in more exposed sea conditions, the freeboard at the bow was raised by giving paddle steamers a forecastle, as on the *Brodick Castle* (1878–1910), which was built for year-round service on the Lower Clyde. She also had an aft saloon raised halfway up between deck levels, abaft the paddles.

Monarch (1888–1951), built for south-coast work, also had a forecastle and, in a further development from the half saloon of the *Brodick Castle*, the whole thing was raised onto main-deck level aft.

It was inevitable that the next design step would be to connect the forecastle to the deck over the machinery and to extend the aft saloon outwards to the full width of the ship, as seen in the *Majestic* (1901–1916). She is pictured here approaching Swanage Pier.

Some paddlers were much altered over the years to suit circumstances. *Lorna Doone* (1891–1948) was built for service on the Bristol Channel, with an open foredeck and one funnel. In 1899, she moved to Southampton, was re-boilered, and emerged with two funnels. However, she was re-boilered again two years later, reverting to one funnel. In 1907, her promenade deck was extended to the bow, as seen in this picture.

Not all paddlers were a great design success. *Emperor of India* (1906–1957) started out at Southampton as the *Princess Royal*; she sat too low in the water, and so had an extra bit of hull inserted amidships to give her more buoyancy.

S.S. "Emperor of India."

She was sold to Cosens of Weymouth in 1908 and they extended the promenade deck to the bow to make her more suitable for long-distance trips, but this re-introduced the weight problem.

After the Second World War, *Emperor of India* was rebuilt out of all recognition, adding yet more weight and making her a very difficult ship to operate, as we will see later.

S.S. "PRINCE OF WALES"

Electricity to provide lighting arrived in the 1880s, but it was very expensive to install and run; it was not until the establishment of the National Grid in the 1930s that its use spread to most homes nationwide. Some steamers were in advance of the curve here. *Prince of Wales* (1891–1938), built for Southampton/Isle of Wight work, had it installed with a steam generator in 1908.

Although the large flush-deck flyers were the prestige flagships of the fleets, their very size made them difficult to fill outside the peak weeks. Consequently, they tended to have short seasons and it was the smaller, and hence more economical, paddlers like the Bristol Channel *Ravenswood* (1891–1955), which started earlier, finished later and clocked up far more operational days each summer.

After the First World War, only a tiny handful of excursion paddle steamers were built for private operators in the UK. One was the *Medway Queen* (1924–present), built for Capt. Shippick's expanding tripping business, based on the Medway and Thames.

One of the smaller paddle steamers was the *Kingswear Castle* (1924–present). Like her consorts on the Dart and other rivers around the UK, she was exceptionally economical to operate in comparison with her larger seagoing cousins, with an ability to carry a payload of 500 passengers (yes, it must have been a squash) using a crew of just four. You can still take a trip on her today on the River Dart.

Princess Elizabeth was built of an economical size for the triple role of excursions in summer, tendering liners in the Solent and for the Southampton–Cowes ferry year round, for which her old-fashioned open foredeck was handy in accommodating those new-fangled things called cars.

The 1930s saw a flurry of paddle-steamer building for the railway companies on the Clyde, Humber and Solent. *Ryde* (1937–present) was built for the Southern Railway's Portsmouth–Ryde service and excursions, and had improved weather protection for the passengers, including an additional saloon with windows on the upper promenade deck to keep the chill out.

The *Lincoln Castle* (1939–2011) was built for the London & North East Railway's ferry connection between Hull and New Holland, and for some excursion work on the Humber. Along with her similar and slightly older sisters, *Tattershall Castle* (1934–present) and *Wingfield Castle* (1934–present), she is an example of how paddle-steamer design moved on to accommodate changes in the wider world. The aft part of the main deck was given over for the carriage of cars.

The final development of the large seagoing excursion paddle steamer came just after the Second World War, with the building of the *Bristol Queen* (1946–1968), pictured, and her near sister *Cardiff Queen* (1947–1969) for service on the Bristol Channel. They were big, fast, well appointed, had loads of undercover accommodation, were of robust construction and were designed to take the worst that the swell sweeping in from the Atlantic could throw at them.

The very last excursion paddle steamer to be built for service in the UK was the *Maid of the Loch* (1952–present), seen here at Balloch. Put together on her own slipway on Loch Lomond, she ran up and down the loch until 1981 and is still with us today, with plans afoot to return her to service.

Chapter 2

View the Military from Bournemouth, 1899

In the first week of August 1899, trips were offered from Bournemouth Pier on the *Monarch, Victoria, Empress, Cynthia* and *Lord Elgin.* On Tuesday, you could have paddled along the Dorset coast to Weymouth, 'Passing through the Fleet of Warships just returned from summer manoeuvres'. On Wednesday, there was 'an afternoon Excursion Passing through the Channel Fleet assembled in the Portland Roads'. On Thursday, a trip 'Round the Isle of Wight' offered a call at Ryde for three hours to see a 'Review of the Hampshire and Isle of Wight Volunteers (over 400) by Her Majesty Queen Victoria'. On Friday, you could have sailed for a 'Grand Cruise' around Portsmouth Harbour to witness the attractions of this 'Important Naval Port, Nelson's famous Flagship *Victory* and the *Terrible*, the largest and most powerful cruiser in the world'.

If all this sightseeing of the instruments of war was not enough, on Saturday it was all aboard for a cross-Channel trip to see what our foreign cousins were up to in 'the French Port and Arsenal' (note the word 'arsenal') of Cherbourg.

It is perhaps small wonder that the previous Saturday offered lighter fare, with a twilight cruise accompanied by the Bournemouth Black and White Minstrels, who performed in a concert-party style that would have to wait another eighty years before its tuneful whimsy would be banned by a less military-minded but more proscriptive society.

Monarch approaching Bournemouth Pier.

Victoria at Lulworth Cove.

Empress (pictured) was of similar appearance to *Cynthia* (1892–1932). The latter ended her career in 1932 when she was blown ashore and wrecked in a gale in Dun Laoghaire Harbour.

Lord Elgin (1876–1955) backing out from Bournemouth Pier.

Chapter 3

All Aboard for Alderney, 1906

This postcard of the *Monarch* off Alderney, on a day trip from Bournemouth and Swanage, is dated 1906 and addressed to Eve Parfitt at 189 Newbridge Hill, Bath. On it, Fred wrote, 'We are on this boat out in the Channel. It's very cold indeed but not such a bad trip.'

Cold it might have been that day, but the temperature dropped further in June 1940, when the German army invaded and turned Alderney into a fortress. At its peak, there were around 5,000 slave labourers, including the sixteen-year-old Anton Yezhel, mostly from Russia and the Ukraine, housed in four concentration camps on the island. Many died from starvation, being overworked, disease or execution.

Looking at Alderney today with its pleasant new locals, with their pleasant new houses, often with pleasant new greenhouses, it is hard to imagine the sheer horror and terror that existed on that island almost eighty years ago. How can it be that, at one moment, day trippers from Bournemouth on the *Monarch* can be touring amiably on a charabanc merry with the laughter of children and then, less than four decades later, on the very same spot, on the very same soil, and on the very same island, sixteen-year-old boys can be imported as slave labourers, subjected to unimaginable cruelty and then shot?

Today, Alderney has moved on. It counts *The Sound of Music* star Julie Andrews as one of its sometime residents, not far from the street down which the adolescent Anton Yehzel once trudged, weighed down, as he must have been, by an ebb tide of just about everything, on his way to the concentration camp.

The last paddle steamer to call at Alderney was the *Helper* (1873–1929) in 1926.

Monarch off Alderney.

Chapter 4

Bristol Channel to the Scilly Isles, 1907

The Bristol Channel benefitted from a number of markets, including the increasing tourist industry in Devon, and the developing industrial hinterland, based on coal, in South Wales with its expanding workforce, ever eager to get afloat on their days off. In 1801, the population of Monmouthshire had been around 45,000. By 1901, it had gone up tenfold to almost half a million, which was music to the ears of excursion paddle-steamer operators.

Local trips centred on Cardiff, Barry and Weston-super-mare, connecting Wales and Devon. A variety of longer cruises were also on offer down the Welsh and Devon coasts and on to the remoteness of Lundy Island, a destination that would have seemed very different in character from the bottom of a pit in the Rhonda Valley.

As steamer operators gained a better understanding of their markets, some of the longest coastal trips were the first to be axed. For example, if you had wanted to go from Cardiff to the Isles of Scilly by paddle steamer, then you would have had to have done it before 1907, when P & A Campbell's *Britannia* made her last call there on a three-day excursion.

Leaving Cardiff and Weston in the morning of the first day, it took until evening for the run down the Bristol Channel, calling at Ilfracombe and going on round Land's End to Penzance, where passengers went ashore for the night. The following morning, the steamer sailed 35 miles out into the Atlantic to the Scilly Isles, arriving in time for lunch, and then sailed back to Penzance for another night ashore. It then set off again on day three, heading back up the channel and home. Inevitably, this was an expensive trip, involving three days of travel and two overnight stops. It was recreated once a year by the *Bristol Queen* from 1963 to 1967.

Britannia (1895–1946).

Chapter 5

Edwardian North Wales, Liverpool and Blackpool

The North Wales and Lancashire coasts benefited from their closeness to the huge population centres in the industrial heartland of the Midlands.

North Wales, S. S. Snowdon

Above: *Snowdon* (1892–1930) was built for the Snowdon Passenger Steamship Company's sailings from Llandudno to Beamaris, Bangor, Menai Bridge and Caernarvon. She passed to the Liverpool & North Wales Steamship Company in 1899 and continued on the same routes, as well as sometimes sailing to Blackpool, until 1930.

Opposite above: The paddle steamer *Lune* (1892–1923), pictured left, was built for the London & North Western Railway services from Blackpool and Fleetwood. She was bought by Cosens in 1913 for service at Weymouth and renamed *Melcombe Regis*, ending her career in 1923. The paddle steamer on the right is *Greyhound* (1895–1936), built for the North Pier Steamship Company of Blackpool. She ran longer excursions from the resort to Llandudno and the Isle of Man, as well as more occasional connections to Liverpool and Preston. She was sold in 1923 for further use as a tender and for excursions on Belfast Lough, but a boiler accident the following year put a stop to that. She was sold on for service in Constantinople under the new name of *Buyuk Ada*.

Above: The giant *La Marguerite* (1894–1925) was built for cross-Channel excursion work from the Thames. She moved north in 1904, sailing from Liverpool to Llandudno and the Menai Straits until 1925. Here she is 'stern fetching' at Bangor. It is best practice to head into the tide when berthing, but on a narrow river turning round to do this is often easier said than done. In this manoeuvre, *La Marguerite* has the tide behind her (see the yachts on the other side lying to the tide), has gone slightly past the pier, and angled her stern across the tide. She is now going full astern (see the paddle wash) and will back into the pier, stemming the tide with her stern.

Chapter 6

Capt. Shippick Forges New Medway Trips, 1920/30s

The young Capt. Shippick had his ship *Brodick Castle* sold out from under him after boiler trouble developed in 1910. This bit of bad news for him had a seismic effect on excursion steamer sailings on the Thames and Medway in later years.

He left Cosens and set up his own business in 1913, first with the small, clinker-built paddle steamer *Advance* (1904–1913), which he renamed *Studland Belle,* and then the following year with the *Audrey* (1897–1929), running local trips from Bournemouth.

During the First World War, he and the *Audrey* moved to the Medway on charter for government work. After this, he snapped up the assets of the old Medway Steam Packet Co. and, with his excellent commercial acumen, expanded the business.

In 1924, he ordered the paddle steamer *Medway Queen* and, among other paddlers, bought two enormous former Admiralty Ascot-class paddle minesweepers, HMS *Melton* (1916–1951) and HMS *Atherstone* (1916–1952) in 1928. These he converted into passenger paddle steamers and renamed *Queen of Thanet* and *Queen of Kent.*

These turned out to be big revenue generators on the cross-Channel trips to France. This stoked up enough background finance to give sufficient confidence to investors (including shipbuilders Denny of Dumbarton) to go ahead and build the first of the giant, ultra-modern, diesel and all-weather Thames excursion vessels: *Queen of the Channel* (1935–1940). She was followed by *Royal Sovereign* (1937–1940) and *Royal Daffodil* (1939–1967).

Capt. Shippick succeeded Capt. Tilsed as master of the *Brodick Castle* in 1908.

Capt. Shippick's first real success story, *Audrey*.

Capt. Shippick's second success story, *Medway Queen*.

One of Capt. Shippick's big revenue generators, *Queen of Kent*.

Royal Daffodil was a far cry from the antiquated *Brodick Castle* with her limited covered accommodation, on which Capt. Shippick had started out.

Chapter 7

Sussex Coast, 1927

P & A Campbell used various paddle steamers from their fleet to run services on the Sussex coast from Brighton, Eastbourne, Hastings, Newhaven and Worthing from the 1890s through to 1956.

In the week commencing Saturday 12 June 1927, *Devonia* (1905–1940) ran the cross-Channel trips to Boulogne. She started the day at Newhaven and picked up at Brighton around 9.30 a.m., before sailing on to leave Eastbourne at 11 a.m.

On Tuesday 14 June, *Devonia* was scheduled to leave Eastbourne at 12 noon for a cruise to Hastings, giving an hour and a half ashore. This was followed by an afternoon cruise eastwards towards Dungeness, before returning to Eastbourne at 5 p.m.

Also on Tuesday 14 June, *Waverley* (1907–1941, one of several paddle steamers with this name) started the day at Newhaven and sailed light to Hastings for a 9 a.m. start. She then picked up at Eastbourne at 9.50 a.m., with a further call at Brighton for a day trip westwards to Sandown. On Wednesday 15, she came up to Eastbourne from Brighton to offer a 4.20 p.m. 'Afternoon Cruise round the *Royal Sovereign* Lightship', before setting off back to Brighton at 5.30 p.m.

On Thursday 16, she was scheduled to leave Eastbourne at 10.30 a.m. for a three-hour coastal trip eastwards to Folkestone, after an earlier pick up at Brighton at 9 a.m. She called at Hastings on the way, giving two hours ashore at the Kent port with a return time to Eastbourne of 6 p.m.

It was the *Brighton Belle* that was the local paddle steamer doing the rounds of the piers that week as usual, with the odd excursion 'Towards Seaford Bay', 'Round the *Royal Sovereign* Lightship', and to Newhaven 'to witness the arrival of the Mail Steamer' thrown in.

Most people didn't have passports in those days, but nonetheless had to satisfy the purser that they were British or French citizens for trips to Boulogne. This, along with HM Customs requirements, sometimes produced difficulties. In August 1927, a chartered accountant was convicted of trying to smuggle ashore at Hastings one bottle of brandy and another of eau de cologne. He had also been seen to throw two more bottles overboard, which the customs officer on the pier thought were perfume, on which duty should have been paid.

In September 1928, a teacher travelled from Brighton to Boulogne on *Devonia*, having bought two tickets and handed one over in France to an Italian acquaintance. At Boulogne, it was found that the numbers of tickets issued and passengers going ashore did not tally, so a strict search was made and the two men were arrested. The Italian received a sentence of a month's hard labour for landing in the United Kingdom without permission and the teacher a fine.

Brighton Queen (1905–1940) was built as the *Gwalia* for Bristol Channel work and spent many summers operating from Brighton. She was sunk while evacuating troops from Dunkirk.

Brighton Belle (1900–1940) was also sunk at Dunkirk. So ubiquitous was her presence over many years at Brighton that she secured a place in the memory of those not even remotely interested in the history of excursion paddle steamers by getting a mention in Graham Greene's novel *Brighton Rock*. She featured as a suitable location for Ida and Mr Corkery to have a drink when the pubs ashore were shut.

Chapter 8

Scarborough Bust-Up, 1928

The paddle steamer *Bilsdale* (1900–1934) started life as the *Lord Roberts* for the Great Yarmouth Steam Tug Company's excursion services along the Norfolk coast. She was chartered to Cosens in 1911 and 1912, before taking up work in the war as the *Earl Roberts*. After that, she was bought by Furness Shipbuilders for work on the Tees and, in 1924, sold on to Crosthwaite Shipping to run excursions from Scarborough.

They renamed her *Bilsdale* and put her into service, with a schedule generally consisting of short trips along the coast off Hayburn Wyke and occasionally to Bridlington. Scarborough was a busy resort, and there was great competition between rival boat businesses and local boatmen, which was exacerbated by the harbour being tidal. To get the best trade, everyone wanted to use the best berth, which was the one that had the best water on it for the longest period. When the tide was low, there was not a lot of water anywhere in the harbour. When the tide was up, the berth closest to the shore was preferred, so that potential passengers could be picked off first.

Inevitably, disputes arose, and sometimes these could be acrimonious and violent. In August 1928, some of the *Bilsdale*'s crew became involved in a brawl with local fishermen after an evening drinking session ashore. This resulted in one of the deckhands falling into the harbour and hitting his head on the way down. Sadly, the poor man died from his injuries and two Scarborough boatmen were charged with murder. This charge was later reduced to manslaughter, with the pair eventually being bound over for three years to keep the peace.

1934 saw further competition — this time from the brand-new *Royal Lady* (1934–1942). Freshly built by John Crown & Sons of Sunderland, she was powered by diesel and had much enhanced facilities, sweeping the board. The *Bilsdale* made her last trip on 17 September 1934 before retiring defeated and sailing no more.

The white-hulled *Bilsdale* off Scarborough, where she ran short excursions for a decade from 1924.

Aboard the *Bilsdale* on a cruise from Scarborough in August 1928 with (from left to right) Winston (aged fifteen), Edwin, Mary (aged nine) and Edith Megoran. Winston became a marine artist and died in 1971. Edwin, an inspector of taxes, remarried in 1939 and died in 1950. Mary became a school teacher in Acton and died in 1994. Edith died in 1938.

In the stern of the *Bilsdale*, with Edith showing more interest in her book than the trip itself.

The harbour at Scarborough in 1934, with the *Bilsdale* on the left and the newly arrived competitor *Royal Lady* ahead of her.

Chapter 9

Thames Toffs, 1935

In the summer of 1935, Londoners had the opportunity to sail down the Thames from Tower Pier every day, excepting Fridays, to Southend, Margate, Ramsgate or Clacton on any one of three huge paddle steamers: *Golden Eagle* (1909–1951), *Crested Eagle* (1925–1940) and the *Royal Eagle* (1934–1954). With a gross tonnage of 1,539 tons, the *Royal Eagle* was a massive ship and more than twice the size of today's *Waverley* (1947–present).

Each paddler was marketed with their own slogan. The *Royal Eagle* was 'London's Own Luxury Liner'; the *Crested Eagle* was the 'Greyhound of the River'; and the *Golden Eagle* was styled as the 'Happy Ship'.

The *Eagle Steamer* handbook explained:

> The slogan we have adopted may cause people to wonder what difference can be made between ships going on afternoon cruises to sea. We lay claim that, once you are aboard the *Golden Eagle*, there is not a dull moment. Sports and games start immediately on leaving the pier; the kiddies find real fun and enjoyment in the balloon-blowing competitions, skipping, musical chairs, tug of war and streamer throwing. Even the grown-ups cannot be kept out; they become young once again and want to blow balloons and enter into the fun with all the keenness of the youngsters. Soon all are one great big happy family, hence our slogan, 'The Happy Ship'.

First away each summer day of 1935 was the 'Happy Ship', the *Golden Eagle*. She set off from Tower Pier at 8 a.m. (workers' hours) and called at Greenwich, North Woolwich and Southend for arrival at Margate at 12.30 p.m. From there she ran an afternoon cruise before coming back.

Second away at 9 a.m. was the 'Greyhound of the River', the *Crested Eagle*. She took the longest trip, all the way to Clacton, where she was scheduled to arrive at 2.15 p.m. before undertaking another short cruise and returning.

Last away at 9.20 a.m. (gentlemen's hours) was 'London's Own Luxury Liner', the *Royal Eagle*. She called at Greenwich, North Woolwich, Tilbury, Southend and Margate, before proceeding on to Ramsgate.

The leaflet also shows that the transport economics fare structure of the budget airlines today was already in existence on the Thames steamers in the 1930s. For example, it would have cost you 10*s* (or 12*s* if you had chosen to sit on the exclusive sun deck both ways) to sail from London to Margate and back on 'London's Own Luxury Liner' on a Saturday or a Sunday. This was quite a lot of money at the time, but you could have done the same trip on the same ship for only 8s during the week. If you had chosen to slum it aboard the 'Happy Ship' and take advantage of all the balloon blowing and skipping, you would have got the same return trip to Margate for a mere 4s during the week. However, you would have had to stump up 5s for it on a Saturday and to dig even deeper into your pocket on a Sunday when the fare rocketed up to 8s, the same price the toffs were paying for 'London's Own Luxury Liner' during the week. With a keen commercial acumen, the company set the prices according to the level of demand for any cruise, and to the size of the pockets of the different market segments that they were targeting.

'Greyhound of the River' *Crested Eagle* and 'London's Own Luxury Liner' *Royal Eagle* alongside Southend Pier in the 1930s.

The 'Happy Ship', *Golden Eagle*.

Chapter 10

Torquay Taster, 1936

Apart from some competition in the 1920s from Cosens's *Alexandra* (1879–1934), and occasional competition from larger paddle steamers at other times, the *Duchess of Devonshire* (1892–1934) and *Duke of Devonshire* were the mainstay of coastal excursions from Exmouth and Torquay right through to the early 1930s. At this time, their fortunes declined and they were withdrawn. The *Duchess of Devonshire* reappeared in private ownership on her old routes in 1933 and 1934, but came to an unfortunate end, as we will see later.

After a spell in Ireland, the *Duke of Devonshire* reappeared at Torquay in 1936 and 1937 under the management of Capt. J. R. Radley, and commenced her new service from the Princess Pier on Tuesday 15 June 1936 with a day excursion to Plymouth, leaving at 10.30 a.m. and returning at 8 p.m. This trip was the most exposed to weather that these paddlers undertook, as it involved sailing round Start and Prawle Points, from which a heading up to Plymouth put them broadside on to the prevailing south-westerly wind. It often lead to much rocking and rolling.

On Wednesday 16 June, there were morning and afternoon cruises at 10.45 a.m. and 2.30 p.m. for time ashore in Dartmouth, followed by an hour-and-a-half evening cruise at 8.15 p.m., viewing Teignmouth, Dawlish and Babbacombe Bay.

On Thursday 17 June, there was a day trip to Lyme Regis, leaving at 10.45 a.m. and returning at 6.45 p.m. This included a short trip from Lyme Regis at 2.15 p.m. The run across Lyme Bay was generally more comfortable than the trip to Plymouth, as the course was out with the prevailing south-westerly wind directly astern and ahead on the return, which reduced rolling. However, there is not a lot of water in the harbour at Lyme Regis, so there was always the danger of grounding there around low tide in the early afternoon. The *Princess Elizabeth* got stuck there twice in 1961.

On Saturday 19 June, there were morning, afternoon and evening cruises to see the yachts taking part in an International Regatta off Torquay. On Sunday 20 June, there was an afternoon cruise leaving Torquay at 2.30 p.m. to land passengers over the bow and onto the beaches at Seaton and Sidmouth, with a return home at 10 p.m.

In 1938, *Duke of Devonshire* was sold to Cosens of Weymouth and renamed *Consul*.

Duke of Devonshire loading passengers over the bow from the beach at Sidmouth.

Aboard the *Duke of Devonshire*.

Duke of Devonshire entering the harbour at Dartmouth.

Cosens's *Alexandra* at Lyme Regis sporting the 'C' on her funnel, painted to distinguish her from her rivals.

Chapter 11

Weymouth Full House, 1949

1949 was the apotheosis of post-war paddle-steamer excursions from Weymouth, with no fewer than four steamers – *Consul*, *Embassy*, *Empress* and *Victoria* – based at the port in the peak weeks. A fifth, the palatial *Emperor of India*, visited from time to time to offer a one-hour cruise 'Round HM Ships and Merchant Shipping in Portland Harbour' in the early afternoon. Meanwhile, a sixth, the *Monarch*, left in the spring for her Bournemouth season and returned in the autumn to lay up for the winter. Never again would there be such a concentration of paddle steamers at Weymouth, or such a diversity of regular trips from it.

The chief excitement of the season was the return to service of the *Consul*. She had been given back to Cosens after the war in poor condition, and it had been touch and go as to whether she would be scrapped. Fortunately, she was rebuilt and returned to service on Whit Monday, 6 June, leaving Weymouth at 10.15 a.m. for Bournemouth and returning at 7.45 p.m.

Towards the end of June, the *Emperor of India,* which, because of her vast size and commensurate running costs, always had the shortest season of any of Cosens's paddlers, started at Bournemouth. This released the *Embassy* to return to Weymouth to become the long distance and 'special' steamer for the peak weeks. Her first trip in this role was on Tuesday 28 June, with a 'Special Tea Cruise to the Bill of Portland' at 2.30 p.m.

The following day, the *Consul* left Weymouth at 9.30 a.m. for Swanage, picking up passengers there for Lulworth Cove. The *Embassy* set off at 10 a.m. for Yarmouth, Isle of Wight, with the smaller *Empress* and *Victoria* filling in on the local trips to Lulworth Cove, Portland Harbour, the Shambles lightship and the Bill of Portland, as required. This set the pattern of sailings for the summer.

In this season of exceptional paddle-steamer activity at Weymouth, with so many paddle steamers to fill, *Embassy* revived the occasional, and very long, day trips to destinations that had previously been dropped, including Torquay, Shanklin and Cowes.

It was a summer of unusually fine weather, with plenty of sunshine and balmy days, and the season ran on until Sunday 9 October. In the years after 1949, it was downhill all the way, with the excursion programmes not helped by indifferent weather for most of the 1950s. The next really baking summer did not come until 1959, by which time paddle-steamer services had reduced dramatically and only one paddler, *Consul*, was offering trips from Weymouth.

The newly refurbished *Consul* backing out of Lulworth Cove.

Embassy in 1952.

Empress alongside at Weymouth in 1950.

Victoria arriving at Bournemouth Pier in 1952.

Emperor of India alongside the Pleasure Pier, Weymouth in 1952.

The first *Monarch*, with twin funnels, backing out from Swanage Pier in 1949.

Chapter 12

Paddle-Steamer Economics, Portsmouth Style, 1951

At 244 feet in length, *Whippingham* was a massive paddle steamer, too large to be filled on regular excursion work, but a boon in shifting the summer crowds on the railway connection between Portsmouth and Ryde. On Saturday 18 August 1951, she carried 4,669 passengers to the Isle of Wight and brought 5,412 back. At today's Wightlink day return fare of £18.40, that would be a cool £92,000 revenue. At the period return rate of £25, it would be an even tastier £125,000. Compare that with 600 passengers on a day excursion at £30 per head, producing just £18,000.

Whippingham (1930–1962) and her sister *Southsea* (1930–1941) were the largest paddle steamers ever built for excursion and ferry work on the south coast.

Chapter 13

Bournemouth Mix-Up, 1957

During the peak weeks, the *Embassy* ran the longer Isle of Wight sailings from Bournemouth, while the second *Monarch* ran the Swanage service. The latter finished in time for a departure from Bournemouth to either Poole directly or to Poole via Swanage, leaving at 6 p.m. The Isle of Wight service finished in time for a departure from Bournemouth to either Poole directly or to Poole via Swanage at 6.30 p.m. This meant that, on some days, the last sailing for Swanage left Bournemouth at 6 p.m. and on other days at 6.30 p.m.; on Wednesdays, because of the scheduling to even up the crew hours between the two ships, it alternated week and week about.

I think that you may already have guessed where this is going. Hundreds of passengers, who planned to sail from Bournemouth to Swanage on the 6.30 p.m. boat on 21 August 1957, arrived to find the *Monarch* half way across the bay on her way to Swanage, having sailed at 6 p.m. It was reported that the steamer notice advertised both departures, and that the blackboard was misleading. Cdr T. Johnson, the local manager, said that this had led to a rumour being spread that the company was about to 'fold up', which was not true. He explained that the reason for the steamer muddle was a printer's error on the schedule, and that this had been chalked up on the blackboard.

The second *Monarch* (1924–1961, previously *Shanklin*) in Weymouth Harbour in the 1950s, with the bow of the *Consul* on the left and the *Embassy* astern.

Embassy alongside at Poole. The long stick attached to her funnel was installed in 1954 to carry a second steaming light, as required by new BOT regulations. Instead of buying and fitting a main mast to carry this, the stick was a cheaper and easier alternative. Cosens were ever parsimonious in keeping costs down.

Chapter 14

Jeanie Deans Bows Out, 1964

In 1964, there were still four paddle steamers operating on the Clyde: *Jeanie Deans* (1931–1968), *Waverley* (1947–present), *Caledonia* (1934–1980) and *Talisman* (1935–1967). *Jeanie Deans* was designed primarily for the LNER route from Craigedoran to Arrochar, although she did spend much of the 1930s on longer services to lower parts of the Clyde. After the Second World War, she was given a major rebuild, and this final design was used as the basic template for the slightly smaller paddle steamer *Waverley* of 1947, which remains with us today.

With food rationing still in force and materials of all kinds in short supply, building a new passenger paddle steamer of any quality in a climate of austerity was easier said than done. There were those who felt that the new *Waverley* was not quite the equal of the paddle steamer on which she was based.

The new ship was given a slightly more modern profile than the *Jeanie Deans*, including a raked bow and a cruiser stern, and she sat lower in the water, giving her less freeboard under the sponsons. She also turned out to have less favourable handling characteristics than many paddle steamers, with a distinct tendency to back into the wind when steaming astern and a marked propensity for the bow to fall in on piers while berthing.

It was, therefore, the *Caledonia*, with her better construction, better handling characteristics and more seagoing abilities, that was the preferred Ayr excursion steamer for sailings in the lower Clyde, and to sea by 1964.

The diesel-electric paddler *Talisman* was the ferry workhorse, and spent pretty much the whole 1964 summer running backwards and forwards on the Wemyss Bay–Millport ferry service.

After slipping at Lamont's Shipyard at Port Glasgow in March 1964, *Jeanie Deans* emerged in April with both a mere six-month extension to her passenger certificates and the news that as little money as possible had been spent on her, as she was to be withdrawn at the end of the season. She started on 9 May with a charter, and commenced her main excursion programme on Sunday 7 June. This lasted into September, with her schedule in the peak weeks alternating with the *Waverley*.

One week, *Waverley* operated the afternoon cruise, leaving at 12.40 p.m. and returning at 6.50 p.m. It went from Craigendoran, through the Kyles, and round Bute each day from Sundays to Fridays. Meanwhile, the *Jeanie Deans* ran the longer day trips to Brodick and the cruise to Pladda on Mondays; trips to Lochgoilhead and Arrochar on Tuesdays and Thursdays; visits 'Round the Lochs and Firth of Clyde' on Wednesdays; and a cruise up river to Glasgow, with time ashore, on Fridays. The following week, the two ships swapped over to balance the crew hours. On Saturdays, they usually ran the ferry service to Rothesay, either from Wemyss Bay or from Craigendoran.

As the season wound down in September, *Jeanie Deans* operated various ferry services as required and continued with some excursions, making her last trip with passengers on Monday 28 September. The following morning, she sailed to the Albert Harbour, Greenock, for lay-up and so ended her Clyde excursion career.

Jeanie Deans had two large promenade deck shelters and two large saloons on the main deck, giving much more covered accommodation than her predecessors.

Waverley, in early November 1965, in the Albert Harbour, Greenock. She is berthed alongside the Macbrayne turbine steamer *King George V* (1926–1984) with the funnels of the *Jeanie Deans* on the left, which was about to set off for the Medway.

Caledonia was built for summer and winter work to sea in the lower Clyde. She was withdrawn in 1969 and, after a spell on the Thames as a restaurant and bar, she caught fire and was scrapped in 1980.

The diesel-electric paddler *Talisman* alongside in the Albert Harbour, Greenock, in November 1965. She was withdrawn the following year.

Chapter 15

Humber Scene, 1965 and Before

The paddle steamers built to maintain the ferry service across the Humber between Hull and New Holland also operated excursions in the summer from Hull to view the docks, and from Grimsby to Spurn Head and up river to Hull. They did not have seagoing passenger certificates, and so did not ply beyond the partially smooth water limit, which was an imaginary line linking Cleethorpes Pier and Patrington Church, just inside Spurn Head.

Doncaster (1856–1914) ran the Hull/New Holland ferry service and some excursions with her near sister *Liverpool* (1855–1905) until 1914. Beyond her are the local steamers *Empress* (1893–1930) from Goole and *Her Majesty* (1858–1912) from Ferriby Sluice, both owned by the Hull & Goole Steam Packet Co.

Victoria Pier, Hull

Killingholme (1912–1945) was built for the Great Central Railway ferry service between Hull and New Holland and must surely be among the oddest paddle steamers ever built, with her giant funnel and double-ended construction. She is seen here brand new at Hull and is painted white for a visit of King George V in 1912. The smaller steamer on the left is the *Doncaster*.

Lincoln Castle, pictured alongside at Hull in August 1965 sporting the then-brand-new railway double-arrow symbol on her funnel. She was built in 1940 on the Clyde and operated on the ferry service between Hull and New Holland until 1978, as well as being used for excursions. She was of a slightly different design to her near sisters *Tattershall Castle* and *Wingfield Castle*, with a slightly shallower draught that gave her an edge in crossing the Humber shallows at low water springs. However, when berthing alongside piers, this made her more of a handful for her captains, some of whom preferred to be rostered on the other two paddlers. After being withdrawn, *Lincoln Castle* had a new career as a floating bar, first near the Humber Bridge and then at Grimsby, before being scrapped in 2011.

Deck view of *Lincoln Castle* showing the huge width of the bridge, which extended across the full breadth of the ship over the paddles. Just abaft the bridge on the promenade deck is a rail with its sign dividing the deck area between first- and second-class passengers. This was a two-class railway ship.

Lincoln Castle's car deck in 1965.

Chapter 16

One Paddle Steamer Life:
Lord Elgin

Lord Elgin was built in 1876 by Richardson Duck & Co. of Stockton-on-Tees, with machinery by T. Richardson & Sons of Hartlepool, for the services of Galloway, Kidd & Watson of Leith on the Firth of Forth. In 1881, she was acquired by the newly formed Bournemouth, Swanage & Poole Steam Packet Company for their services from the recently rebuilt Bournemouth Pier at this expanding resort, which had hardly existed as a town only a few years before. Indeed, when the railway extended from Southampton to Dorchester in 1847, it bypassed Bournemouth altogether, instead being routed to the north via Ringwood and Wimborne.

Lord Elgin was such a success that her owners ordered a new and larger steamer, *Bournemouth* (1884–1886). Unfortunately, she had a very short career – as we will see later – and was replaced by the *Brodick Castle*, plus another new arrival: the even more commodious and coal-hungry *Windsor Castle* (1891–1931).

These paddlers operated in competition with Cosens & Co., although arrangements between the two companies became harmonious, with *Brodick Castle* eventually passing into Cosens' fleet. In 1896, the company was reconstituted as the Bournemouth & South Coast Steam Packet Company and, from 1899, they operated a joint service from Bournemouth to Swanage with Cosens.

It therefore came as an unwelcome surprise to Cosens in 1909 to find that the *Lord Elgin* had been sold from under their noses to their arch rivals: the Southampton, Isle of Wight & South of England Royal Mail Steam Packet Company (later Red Funnel Steamers). They retained her on the Bournemouth station, now in direct competition with Cosens, for a further two years.

In 1911, Red Funnel converted *Lord Elgin* into a cargo steamer, adding a giant derrick and upright funnel, and transferred her to Southampton for the Cowes ferry service. This she ran regularly, usually making one round trip daily, until September 1952, when her regular place was taken by the roll-on, roll-off vehicle ferry and former tank landing craft *Norris Castle* (1942–1962, eventually sold to Greece).

From 1923 to 1955, *Lord Elgin's* master was Capt. Joe Sewley, who superintended the carriage of all manner of stuff to and from the island. E. P. Leigh-Bennett described the scene aboard in Red Funnel's pre-war guide:

On the after deck, a much-travelled valise (bespattered with old cloak-room tickets), some of Mr Heinz's 57 varieties, a balloon-tyred pram, a drum of wire cable from

Musselborough, a discreet case of ladies' underwear marked 'assorted', four gas stoves, four drums of fish oil for Shanklin's fried fish and chip suppers, a diving board, a portable bungalow and four sides of Danish prime bacon.

On her arrival at Bournemouth in 1881, the almost brand-new and very modern *Lord Elgin* had easily outclassed her competitors as an excursion steamer but, within a decade, larger, faster and more commodious steamers easily excelled her. She went from long-distance luxury excursion steamer, through the local Swanage service, and on to humble cargo ship, in a tale of stately decline that might have popped straight out of the pages of the Rev. Audry's *Thomas the Tank Engine* stories. She quietly plodded backwards and forwards from Southampton to Cowes, carrying everything anyone on the Isle of Wight might ever want (how did they get that portable bungalow aboard?).

Lord Elgin made her last crossing from Cowes to Southampton on 11 May 1955, after which she was moved to Pollock, Brown & Co.'s scrapyard on the River Itchen for demolition, taking with her the ghosts of nearly eighty years of passengers, livestock and assorted parcels.

Lord Elgin in her early days on the south coast. Her captain is on the exposed bridge at the port engine room telegraph, with the ship's wheel on the promenade deck below him and forward of the funnel, an arrangement that was not uncommon on early paddle steamers. The captain therefore had to have a lot of trust in his man on the wheel, particularly when coming alongside piers, as verbal communication between them was not easy, given their distance apart.

Lord Elgin in Pollock & Brown's scrapyard in 1955.

Chapter 17

What It Was Like to Be Aboard the *Monarch* in the 1920s

Let's imagine ourselves back on Bournemouth Pier in the 1920s, about to board the first *Monarch*, which has just arrived for the forty-five-minute trip to Swanage. There is lots of bustle, with people wearing hats and plenty of clothes, even though this is summer.

Back aft in the stern of *Monarch,* in an age before finger-wagging health and safety started bossing everyone about, passengers have made themselves comfortable on the mooring ropes and are mingling around the seaman, who is about to let go.

The aft saloon, which did not extend the full width of the *Monarch,* not only provided refreshing drinks, but also was a good platform from which to take in the view and salty sea air.

Further forward on *Monarch* on the left is the companionway down to the main deck between the two funnels. There were two boiler rooms, one forward and one aft of the machinery. Take note of the boy on the right with the cap and striped tie, and the lady and girl on his right. We'll come back to them later.

The port bridge wing on *Monarch*, with the docking and engine-room telegraphs. The tarpaulin over the paddle box is covering spare deck chairs to increase seating capacity on busy days.

The foredeck. The hatch led down to the crew accommodation, such as it was, in the forecastle below decks, right up in the bow. *Monarch*'s bell, mounted on dolphins, was presented to the Paddle Steamer Preservation Society in 1961.

As at the stern, *Monarch*'s passengers in the bow are sitting and standing with their feet in among the mooring ropes and close to the steam capstan. On Cosens's Bournemouth steamers, tickets were usually sold around the deck rather than from a ticket office. In the foreground is the purser, with his peaked cap and a ticket in his left hand, collecting fares.

Remember the boy with the striped tie, the lady and little girl on the deck of the *Monarch*? Here they are again – Eric, Fanny and Joan Bellamy– this time on the *Bournemouth Queen* (1908–1957). Eric became a Sub-Lt in the RNVR in the Second World War and took the converted trawler HMS *Thrifty* (1916–1946) to Dunkirk. Joan married and her son, Capt. Mike Ledger, became a master with P&O Ferries. There was salt in the family blood.

Chapter 18

What It Was Like to Be Aboard the *Consul* in 1962/63

Looking up at *Consul*'s wheelhouse, which had been painted white instead of being varnished in 1962 after a plywood repair.

Consul's foredeck with its wonderful Victorian domed skylight over the forward saloon, which contained the bar.

Looking up at *Consul*'s bridge. The tank on the right contained firefighting foam for the boiler room.

Consul's port bridge wing, with the engine and docking telegraphs with their covers on.

Mate Arthur Drage wonders why *Consul* is in the wrong place alongside the Pleasure Pier at Weymouth for the gangway to go out. The little chimney by the boat is from the galley range below.

The captain's cabin abaft the funnel shortly after *Consul* had been bought by a consortium, headed by Tony McGinnity, for further service in 1963.

Consul at Lulworth Cove landing passengers over the bow onto the beach.

Looking down onto *Consul*'s aft capstan at Lulworth Cove.

Chapter 19

Food and Drink

Providing food and drink for the passengers was ever a part of paddle-steamer operations, although what was provided and how it was done naturally varied according to the route and length of journey. Short trips might have offered only a very limited fare, while longer ones, particularly those targeted at a wealthy clientele, provided substantial meals.

However, in an age when the majority of people on a day out took a tin sandwich box or a picnic, not everybody wanted a proper lunch aboard and the relatively small dining-saloon capacity of paddle steamers, in comparison with the number of passengers carried, reflected that. For example, even the vast and most luxurious *Royal Eagle* could seat only around 300 for a full meal out of her full complement of up to 2,000.

Galley space was also limited, so many of the bigger companies offering quality food had catering departments ashore, with extensive kitchens where all the real work was done in advance.

As a result, meals on steamers were never cheap. For example, in 1962, on the *Clyde* breakfast was *5s 6d*, luncheon *7s 6d* and high tea *6s*, which compares with *6s 6d* for a four-hour cruise from Millport to Loch Goil on the *Caledonia*, and *13s 3d* for the all-day 'Round of the Lochs and Firth of Clyde' from Largs aboard the *Waverley*. Breakfast or high tea was therefore almost as expensive as the full fare for an afternoon cruise, and lunch was more than half the price of the full day trip; you had to have money to be able to afford both to pay for a trip and to dine aboard.

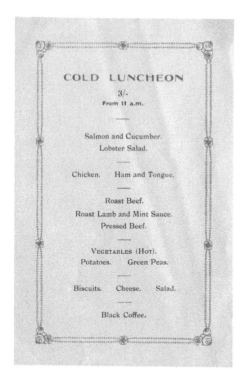

COLD LUNCHEON
3/-
From 11 a.m.

Salmon and Cucumber.
Lobster Salad.

Chicken.   Ham and Tongue.

Roast Beef.
Roast Lamb and Mint Sauce.
Pressed Beef.

VEGETABLES (HOT).
Potatoes.   Green Peas.

Biscuits.   Cheese.   Salad.

Black Coffee.

A menu for a cruise on Cosens's flagship *Majestic* on Saturday 18 July 1914 to view a grand naval pageant, at which HM King George V and HRH the Prince of Wales were to be present. It is a mouth-watering affair with all the different courses, but is actually quite straightforward to prepare, particularly given that it is advertised as a 'Cold Luncheon'. The salmon and cucumber, lobster salad, chicken, ham, tongue and roast beef could all have been prepared in advance, leaving only the vegetables, potatoes, green peas and coffee in need of heating up on the galley range.

The saloon on Red Funnel's Southampton-based *Princess Elizabeth* looking aft towards the doorway, which led into the ladies' lavatory. Red Funnel had a good reputation for catering on their steamers and there was a shore-based catering department where the lobsters were boiled, the beef roasted and the plum tarts baked in readiness for loading aboard their long-distance excursion steamers such as *Lorna Doone*, *Bournemouth Queen* and *Balmoral* (1900–1949).

The dining saloon of the *Medway Queen* set out for lunch. She had a small galley on the main deck, just forward of the boiler room, and continued to prepare a limited range of hot food right up to her last year in service in 1963. After the morning departure from Strood, there was breakfast with bacon, sausage and eggs. For lunch, there was a rib of beef or a leg of lamb, delivered from the local butcher by bicycle that morning and roasted aboard in the ship's oven. For high tea on the way home, there was fish and chips.

The dining saloon on the *Consul* on the first-ever Paddle Steamer Preservation Society charter, an evening cruise from Weymouth on Saturday 10 September 1960. Left to right are Capt. Harry Defrates, John, Winston and Dorothy Megoran, and Ethel Defrates. Capt. Defrates, who that season was the master of the *Monarch*, and is holding up a glass of rum and a copy of issue number 1 of the PSPS journal, *Paddle Wheels*.

The saloon on British Railways's Lymington–Yarmouth paddle steamer *Freshwater* (1927–1962). With a journey time of only half an hour across the Solent to the Isle of Wight, the *Freshwater* never went in for catering in a big way.

At the opposite end of the spectrum, the *Royal Eagle* sailing down the Thames from London to Ramsgate produced the full works of high-end catering, targeting market segments with real money to spend. She had more undercover all-weather accommodation with tables and chairs and picture windows to give a good view of the passing scenery than any other UK excursion paddle steamer ever built. 'Another gin please, steward, and a bowl of crevettes'.

VIEW OF HALF MAIN DINING SALOON: "ROYAL EAGLE"

Royal Eagle's main dining saloon aft could seat 126. There was another dining saloon forward for 100, with 'auxiliary' space for an additional thirty-five on the lower deck aft, plus four private dining rooms for small groups of twelve.

Chapter 20

Captains

Some of the captains came from a deep-sea background, and had Foreign-Going Master's tickets. Others grew up in the coastal trade or on the paddle steamers, and sailed with the equivalent Home-Trade certificates. All of them were superb seaman and ship handlers, safely navigating and berthing their charges in often difficult waters, with complicated tidal patterns. This was without any of the modern kit now deemed to be so essential for ship safety, such as radios, radar, chart plotters, echo sounders, AIS and paper-based safety management systems.

The paddlers carried a lead line, which is a thin rope with a weight on the end that could be thrown over the side to measure the depth of water, to help to understand where they were in fog, and they could trail a rotating log from the stern in order to record the distance travelled on long, particularly cross-channel, sailings. They also had a sextant for working out the distance off headlands and lighthouses; however, expert captains like these sailed backwards and forwards, in and out and up and down coasts, estuaries and rivers, day in and day out. They somehow developed a sort of sixth sense for knowing just where they were, without any general need of recourse to much kit other than that most useful maritime instrument: the human eyeball.

In the early days, the bridges were usually Spartan affairs, with quite low rails and only a small piece of canvas to tuck behind and deflect a bit of the wind and rain. There was a wheel with a rudder indicator on its stand, a binnacle with the compass, engine-room telegraphs to deliver the orders for manoeuvring the engines and, on some paddlers, docking telegraphs to communicate with the deck crew handling the ropes. There was also a voice pipe to the engine room, a wire to pull the whistle for sound signals, a box for the binoculars, a notebook and almanac – and that was about it, with not even a chart table in many cases.

The paddlers carried charts, which were stowed away somewhere in the captains' cabins for use in an emergency, but the masters, who all had local pilotage certificates, were expected to know the charts from memory and to be able to come up with any course and distance, making due allowance for wind and tide, anywhere in their areas, all from their own heads.

Capt. H. J. Hardy on the bridge of the *Monarch*, on a trip from Bournemouth in 1920. He joined Cosens in 1881 as a seaman, but soon worked his way up to become mate and master. He variously commanded the *Albert Victor, Victoria* and *Empress*, and died in 1930.

Capt. W. C. Billy Read on the bridge of the *Alexandra*, alongside at Bournemouth in 1920. He joined Cosens in 1895 and also sailed as master of *Queen, Helper* and *Emperor of India*. He retired in 1935 and was given a bedside table lamp with tassels by his crew.

Capt. H. A. Garnett on the bridge of the *Empress* in 1920. He was also master of the *Albert Victor*, *Queen* and *Monarch*. He died in 1933.

Another shot of Capt. Garnet on the bridge of the *Empress*.

Capt. H. J. Dennis on the bridge of the *Princess Helena* (1883–1952) in 1920, which that year ran Red Funnel's Bournemouth–Swanage service. He joined Red Funnel in 1904 as a deck boy, was promoted to mate in 1910, and subsequently commanded the *Solent Queen, Bournemouth Queen, Lorna Doone* and *Medina*.

Capt. H. F. Defrates, pictured on the *Monarch* in June 1960, was born in London and went to sea in 1910 on colliers trading to South America. During the Second World War, he worked on minesweepers, and later was involved with control of shipping in the Isle of Wight area and with preparations for the Normandy landings. After the war, he joined Cosens as mate of the first *Monarch* and, after sailing as relief master of the *Embassy*, his first permanent command was the *Victoria* in 1951. He was also captain at various times of the *Consul*, the second *Monarch* and the *Princess Elizabeth*. He died in 1984.

Born in 1912, Capt. J. C. W. Iliffe, seen here on the bridge of *Consul* at Weymouth in 1962, went to sea in 1928 and ended up with a Foreign-Going Master's ticket. In 1937, he joined the RNR and took up flying, before being shot down over Norway in 1941 and taken as a prisoner of war. On release, he stayed in the Navy until 1957, when he joined Cosens. Despite being the junior mate, he leap-frogged the others and became captain of the *Consul* in 1960. From 1963 until she was withdrawn in 1966, he was captain of the *Embassy* and so became Cosens's last master. After that, he had several jobs, including selling ice creams from a van at Abbotsbury. He died in 2002.

Capt. Woods, leaning on the docking telegraph of the *Princess Elizabeth* alongside at Weymouth in August 1965, went to sea with Royal Mail Lines on their routes to South America and had a Master's ticket in both steam and sail. At various times, he was captain of the small local passenger vessels *Anzio* at Brighton and *Killoran II* at Torquay, and was master of the *Princess Elizabeth* at Weymouth in 1965. He brought the Clyde paddler *Jeanie Deans* round from the Clyde to the Medway in October 1965, and was her master for the first part of her ill-fated Thames season in 1966.

Capt. Leonard Horsham, seen here on the bridge of the *Medway Queen*, joined the New Medway Steam Packet Co. in the early 1930s as mate of the *Queen of Thanet*. He transferred to the new, ground-breaking diesel passenger vessel *Queen of the Channel* in 1935 and then, in 1937, to the new *Royal Sovereign*. Later that year, he was given his first command, *City of Rochester* (1904–1941). During the war, he commanded the *Thames Queen* (1898–1948) and, after that, was captain of the *Medway Queen* right up to her last sailing in 1963. In common with many of the Thames steamer captains, he sailed as master of the GSN cargo ships on the short sea routes to the near continent in the winter. He died shortly after being taken ill on the *Petrel* (1945–1987) in 1969.

Chapter 21

Engines

Early paddle steamers were fitted with all sorts of weird and wonderful steam machinery but, from the latter part of the nineteenth century, while some were built with oscillating or simple expansion engines, most had diagonal compound reciprocating steam engines. A few of the later and larger steamers had an extra cylinder with triple expansion. Paddle tugs often had two side-lever engines.

The largest paddle steamers carried certificated engineers but, for many steamers of more modest dimensions, the BOT issued exemptions to the skilled company fitters who maintained the engines in winter under the guidance of certificated engineers, allowing them to sail in summer as the chief engineer.

The boiler room of the *Princess Elizabeth*. Originally coal-fired, the *Lizzie*'s boiler was converted to oil after the Second World War, when it became a cheaper fuel. There are three oil burners. The large hinged doors with handles could be lifted up to expose the fire tubes so that they could be swept of soot.

The *Princess Elizabeth's* engine room laid up in 1967.

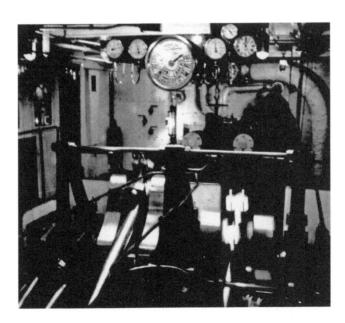

Beyond the main engine of the *Glen Usk* (1914–1963) is the steam steering engine. On some paddlers, this was sited aft next to the rudder; on others, it was in the engine room where it was under the watchful eye of the engineer. In the centre is the engine-room telegraph on 'Full Ahead'. The gauges were for boiler pressure, pressures in the high- and low-pressure cylinders, and the vacuum. These engines developed no power without a good vacuum, which sucked used steam out from the low-pressure cylinder into the condenser to be turned back into water for recirculating into the boiler.

Embassy's engine. The wheel on the bulkhead on the right was for turning the main steam on from the boiler through to the engine. On the rail across the engine are two polished brass oil boxes, with oily wicks hanging down from them. An oil collection tray on the top of each connecting rod brushed past these wicks on each rotation, collecting oil to lubricate the bearings.

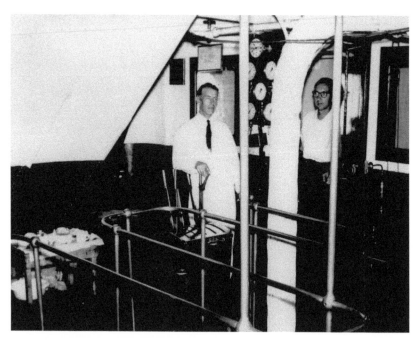

There were five levers for operating the engines on most paddle steamers with compound reciprocating steam engines, like these on the *Freshwater*. One was for ahead or astern, the second for the amount of steam let into the high-pressure cylinder, the third was an impulse valve for injecting steam into the low-pressure cylinder if the engine got stuck, and the other two were cylinder drains to remove any condensate. There were usually other small wheels in the vicinity to control various ancillary steam pumps.

Royal Eagle had one of the largest triple-expansion paddle steamer engines ever built, providing 3,000 ihp, with steam supplied by two oil-fired boilers at a working pressure of 210 psi.

Chapter 22

Independent Paddle Wheels

The overwhelming majority of excursion paddle steamers had one engine connected to both paddle wheels on a fixed shaft, so that both wheels always went the same way at the same time and it was impossible to put one ahead and one astern to turn round short. This has prompted the very commonly held view that paddle steamers were not permitted to have independently operating paddle wheels while carrying passengers, in case they capsized. This seems to be more urban myth than reality, as there were a few paddlers that did have independent wheels, and which did use them independently while carrying passengers.

The *Farringford* (1948–1981) was built for the railway service from Lymington to Yarmouth. Although not looking like everyone's idea of a beautiful paddler, she nevertheless carried passengers and vehicles, had passenger certificates and was propelled by independent paddle wheels, which were operated independently in passenger service.

The Woolwich ferries: *Squires* (1922–1963), *Gordon* (pictured, 1923–1963), *John Benn* and *Will Crooks* (both 1930–1963). All had independent wheels and carried passengers.

The Forth ferries: *Queen Margaret* (pictured, 1934–1964), *Robert the Bruce* (1934–1964), *Mary Queen of Scots* (1949–1964) and *Sir William Wallace* (1956–1964, went to Holland). They also all had independent wheels and carried passengers, as did the Dundee paddler *BL Nairn* (1929–1966) and the Neyland paddler *Cleddau Queen* (1956–1975). The list goes on.

Most of the small harbour and salvage tugs, such as the *Houghton* (1904–1964) pictured here at Sunderland in 1963, had two independent engines, usually side-lever, which could be operated either separately for manoeuvring or coupled together to make sure that they were both going at the same speed when at sea. Many of these paddle tugs also had passenger certificates.

Chapter 23

Survey and Certification

All ships carrying more than twelve passengers had to have a passenger certificate issued by the Board of Trade or its successors. These came in different classes, according to whether the vessels were trading on rivers or beyond that to sea. For example, the Thames down to Gravesend was categorised as 'smooth waters', while estuaries, such as the Thames from Gravesend to an imaginary line drawn from Clacton to Reculver, were called 'partially smooth waters'.

The sort of passenger certificate issued dictated the structure of the ship, its lifesaving apparatus and the number of passengers that could be carried, with fewer passengers being allowed on the same ship going to sea than one on 'partially smooth waters' or on 'smooth waters'. There were further restrictions in numbers on cross-Channel trips.

Each year, every paddle steamer had to be taken out of the water, not only for hull cleaning and painting, but also for survey by the BOT. The boiler had to be opened up, with all the mountings on it removed for inspection. All parts of the machinery also had to be surveyed, usually on a five-yearly cycle.

Over the years, regulations became tighter. For example, after the sinking of the *Titanic*, larger paddle steamers had to carry more lifeboats although, on excursion steamers, these were never intended to accommodate all the passengers. They were instead for the crew to help to coordinate a major incident. Floating seats, called buoyant apparatus, were the main lifesaving kit. Life jackets were also required on longer coastal voyages, although they were not made compulsory for domestic passenger vessels trading only on categorised waters and short distances to sea until the 1990s.

Consul hauled out of the water on Cosens's slipway for survey at Weymouth in 1960.

Getting slots for survey was sometimes easier said than done, as everyone wanted to refit their steamers at the same time in the spring. Here Cosens's *Monarch* and *Embassy* share a dry dock at Southampton in April 1954. There is a plume of steam coming out of the *Embassy*'s funnel as they tested the boiler safety valves. Her bow rudder, for ease of manoeuvring astern, is just visible.

Buoyant apparatus doubling as seats on the deck of the *Medway Queen* in 1961. The theory was that, in the event of the ship sinking, they would float free and passengers in the water would clutch the grab-lines.

Chapter 24

Riding Posts

With paddle wheels sticking out on both sides, the outboard rubbing band around the paddle box could get caught riding over the top of a berth on a very high tide, leaving the steamer hanging off the quay as the tide went away. In this picture, with the *Emperor of India* on the left at Weymouth and the *Premier* and *Albert Victor* on the right, the rubbing band around the *Emperor*'s port paddle box is already at quay level and is only being prevented from riding over the top by the large riding posts fitted to the berth.

In this close-up shot of the second *Monarch* alongside at Weymouth in January 1961, you can see the posts designed to stop the sponson riding over the quay. On really high spring tides, there were times when *Monarch*'s sponson was a couple of feet above quay level in this berth.

When paddle steamers moored alongside each other, there was also a danger that one or other sponson would ride over or under the other, causing damage, particularly when the ships had a changing list as passengers loaded or disembarked. This is the first *Monarch* with *Consul* alongside at Swanage Pier in 1938 or 1939.

In order to prevent sponsons catching up, the steamers carried short poles, sometimes called 'dollies', which could be hung over the side forward and aft of the paddle box. In this picture of the *Consul* arriving at Swanage in August 1952, you can see one of them hooked up and ready to be deployed where necessary, just forward of the paddle box.

Monarch has one of her 'dollies' deployed for berthing alongside the relatively low West Cowes pontoon. Interpreting what is going on in pictures is an ever-absorbing pastime. The wash from the paddle wheels here gives away that the *Monarch* has been backing out from Cowes, but is now going full ahead. Why was she doing that? Look aft of the funnel over the top of the promenade deck and you can see the sail of a yacht getting in the way. The captain is on the port bridge wing next to the engine room telegraph, having rung 'full ahead' to stop the ship and prevent a collision.

Chapter 25

Weather

Weather was ever a problem for excursion paddle-steamer operators. If it was dull or rainy, passengers did not want to sail. If it was too windy, the steamers could not get into the piers. If it was borderline, there was ever the danger of damage. On the days when the weather conspired against them, the steamers were left tied up, earning no revenue.

To illustrate the point, let's have a look at a selection of details taken from the directors' reports in the 1950s accounts of south-coast paddle-steamer operators Cosens & Co.

From the year ending December 1950:

The weather during the season was exceptionally bad and there was rain on approximately 50 days during the running period. In addition, rough seas and strong winds were experienced, which resulted in 14 blank days at Bournemouth, 13 at Weymouth, 15 at Weymouth Beach and 145 trips had to be cancelled. There was a definite falling off in spending power of those who patronised the steamers, due no doubt to the high cost of living, coupled with the International situation, but the greatest blow we encountered was the serious epidemic (of polio) which broke out on the Isle of Wight just at the peak of the season, resulting in the fact that intending passengers simply refrained from travelling to the Island.'

From the year ending December 1951:

During the season the Company had not only to contend with rising prices of fuel, wages and stores but the weather was extremely bad. There were 30 days when it was impossible to run from Bournemouth and no less than 60 trips to Lulworth Cove were cancelled.

From the year ending December 1954:

The weather was almost the worst on record. Weather experts tell us it was the wettest since 1946, the coldest since 1920 and the least amount of sunshine since 1912. So far as the company are concerned there were 13 blank days at Bournemouth and 49 trips had to be cancelled while at Weymouth there were 8 blank days, 71 trips to Lulworth Cove had to be cancelled.

From the year ending December 1956:

> With the high cost of preparing ships for a limited period of service, constantly increasing operating costs and having to depend on weather conditions, it is becoming increasingly uncertain whether pleasure steamer services can any longer be operated remuneratively and the advisability of discontinuing them completely has been carefully considered. Assured however of the full cooperation of Bournemouth Corporation it has been decided to continue services in 1957. They will, however, be restricted to the peak holiday months and two ships only, the *Monarch* and the *Embassy* will operate from Bournemouth. The *Consul* will also be operated for a further season from Weymouth. Following this decision the *Emperor of India* was sold early in January 1957.

From the year ending December 1960:

> The Company's steamer services were again adversely affected by exceptionally bad weather experienced, which contributed to the reduction in the overall Trading Profit. Your Directors have decided to further reduce the pleasure steamer services and, during the summer of 1961, the *Embassy* only will be stationed at Bournemouth and the *Monarch* sold for scrap.

Embassy and *Monarch* tied up alongside Poole Quay on an inclement day in 1951, rather than being out at Bournemouth earning money.

Emperor of India laid up in the Backwater at Weymouth.

Monarch alongside the Pleasure Pier in
Weymouth in March 1961, awaiting a tug
to tow her to the scrapyard in Cork.

Chapter 26

Fog

Before radar, fog was the mariner's nightmare. Navigating through it required setting a course with due allowance for wind and tide, measuring the distance to be travelled and – taking account of the speed – working out how long it would take to get there. During the voyage, eyes were used in the bow and on the bridge to peer through the gloom, and ears to listen for sound signals from other ships, navigation buoys, land-based stations and anything else. For example, the sound of children playing would have indicated that you were close to a beach or pier. The depth of water could also have been taken by swinging the lead.

When the distance had been run, in theory the ship should have been at its correct destination and, if that was a steamer pier, then hopefully there was the pier bell being rung on which to home in. If in doubt, there was only one safe thing to do: go to anchor and wait for the mists to clear.

With 125 excursionists aboard, the Red Funnel paddle steamer *Balmoral* spent the night of 3 August 1937 at sea in fog. She left Southampton for Bournemouth and Cherbourg, and was due back at Southampton at 10 p.m. However, on the way back from Bournemouth in the evening, she ran into thick fog near the Needles and had to remain anchored until 5 a.m., when she groped her way up Southampton Water to the Royal Pier, arriving at 7.45 a.m. The *Echo* reported, 'Everybody kept cheerful and made the best of the situation. Lifebelts were used as mattresses on deck'.

On 6 July 1958, the *Monarch* found her way to Swanage with some difficulty in the fog and cancelled all her other sailings for the rest of the day, remaining alongside overnight and sending her passengers back to Bournemouth by bus. The *Embassy* (pictured in 1956) got only as far as Bournemouth and overnighted there instead of returning to Poole as scheduled. On 5 June 1965, she came within feet of hitting Ballard Point on a PSPS charter in thick fog.

On 31 August 1961, with ninety aboard, the *Swanage Queen* (previously both *Sussex Queen* and *Freshwater*) couldn't locate Swanage Pier in fog, and so dropped her anchor for the night in the bay. She hauled up the next morning and eventually landed her passengers, who had by then been aboard for twenty-five hours.

Chapter 27

Rescues

Steaming up and down the coast, often inshore, excursion paddle steamers were well placed to assist each other or other craft in distress.

In August 1937, *Bournemouth Queen* rescued two teenage girls, Winifred and Lillian Ticher from Walthamstow, who got lost in fog in a rowing boat off the east coast of the Isle of Wight during their summer holiday at Ventnor. They had gone for a short row, but the current took them out to sea. They tried vainly to get back as fog overwhelmed them and, in desperation, shouted but soon became too hoarse for their voices to carry far. They were overjoyed when they heard the whistle of the *Bournemouth Queen* approaching, as she was cautiously feeling her way around the island. The boat was spotted, the girls taken aboard, and they landed later that afternoon at Cowes.

The paddle steamer *Monarch* spent most of her decade in Cosens's fleet from 1951 running backwards and forwards on the Bournemouth–Swanage service, on which she passed the entrance to Poole Harbour up to ten times a day in the peak weeks. She was therefore well-placed to spot the personal disasters of weekend sailors struggling to get to grips with their sometimes rather less-than-seaworthy craft as they emerged from the safety of the harbour. One such rescue was of Mr and Mrs Spiers and their son, who were plucked from a 30-foot converted lifeboat, which got into difficulty on its way from Poole to Swanage on an inauspicious date, Friday 13 August 1954. An attempt was made to tow the boat to Swanage, but it became waterlogged and sank.

On her cruise from Bournemouth to Totland Bay on 29 August 1954, Capt. Rawle, on the *Emperor of India*, spotted an upturned red dinghy between Hurst Point and the Needles. He went over to take a look but could see no sign of life. Consequently, he continued on his way and reported the incident to the coastguard. It turned out that the dinghy was a 'Sandpiper' cadet craft, which had capsized and its twelve-year-old occupants, Jane Nicholson and Judith Waite, had already been rescued by a boat from Hurst Castle Sailing Club.

In 2 September 1955, Mr Trevor Honnor, aged 22, was out in his boat with his two boys and his mother-in-law off Osmington when the weather freshened, waves swamped his engine and they lost their oars overboard. Fortunately, by waving their jumpers, they managed to attract the attention of Capt. Merryweather on the *Empress,* which is pictured here at Lulworth Cove in 1952, and were brought back safely into Weymouth.

Chapter 28

Breakdowns

Paddle steamers were generally well maintained by crews who understood them, and who had often worked on them over many years; however, breakdowns did occur from time to time.

On an afternoon cruise from Ryde to Bournemouth in 1935, the Southern Railway's almost new *Whippingham*, pictured here berthing at Ryde with Red Funnel's *Gracie Fields* (1936–1940) beyond, broke down off the Needles with 400 passengers aboard on a breezy afternoon. She dropped the anchor, called for assistance, and was attended by rival Red Funnel's *Balmoral* and *Bournemouth Queen*. The latter suffered some damage in trying to come alongside to take off the passengers and so gave up. Red Funnel's tug *Clausentum* (1926–1966) then turned up and offered a tow, but this was declined for fear of a salvage claim. Eventually, another of the Southern Railway's own paddle steamers, *Freshwater*, steamed out to tow her company consort back home.

The *Emperor of India* was a difficult ship, described by her last master, Capt. Rawle, as 'a nightmare for all who had to handle her'. She sat low in the water and her paddle boxes tended to clog up, leading to numerous breakdowns and other difficulties. For example, on the way back to Bournemouth from a trip to Southampton to view the *Queen Mary* in September 1936, with several hundred aboard, one of her wheels fractured, bending a bracket and various rods, and she had to go to anchor. The first *Monarch* was dispatched from Poole to collect the passengers, who arrived back at Bournemouth at 1 a.m. The *Echo* reported, 'Although at first anxious about their suppers, the passengers soon settled down to the spirit of a moonlight adventure and the younger people roused the denizens of the sea with an impromptu concert.'

On returning to the Isle of Wight from a day trip to Cherbourg in 1937, the *Balmoral*, with about 400 aboard, suffered a steering gear failure while trying to berth at Shanklin Pier. She anchored off, the engineers set to work fixing the problem, and it was 3 a.m. before she got home to Southampton. Cross-Channel flyers like the *Balmoral* were subject to the most stresses and strains of all the excursion paddle steamers, with their schedules taking them out onto the high seas and potentially quite heavy weather, which flexed their hulls and machinery and clogged up their paddle boxes, setting up hydraulic pressures of some force on their lightly built constructions. As another example, on 3 September 1929, *Balmoral*'s paddle shaft snapped between Bournemouth and Swanage. She dropped the anchor, passengers were transferred to *Solent Queen*, and she was towed back to Southampton.

In July 1952, *Consul* developed a paddle-wheel problem in Swanage Bay. Passengers were transferred to the second *Monarch* and *Consul* was towed back to Poole.

Chapter 29

Difficult Piers

All seaside piers were weather dependent and had tidal vagaries, which occurred throughout the tidal cycle, thus taxing the skills of the captains. Sometimes, passengers could be picked up in the morning, but the sea would be too rough to drop them back later, forcing them to be carried on to a distant harbour, remote from their seaside lodgings.

With the massive 45-foot rise and fall of tide, combined with exposure to swell coming straight in from the Atlantic, the Bristol Channel piers and harbours presented real challenges for the captains. In this picture, almost all the water has gone away from Ilfracombe. P & A Campbell's *Britannia* (1896–1957) and *Bristol Queen* are lying off.

This may look like an idyllic day, with the *Victoria* alongside Bournemouth Pier, but tides across the pier pushed the steamers on, leading to them land heavily or off, thereby missing the ropes, however much the sun shone.

Some piers had a problem with depths of water and could only be approached one way, irrespective of the direction of the wind or tide. Due to surrounding sandbanks, there was generally only one way in and out of South Parade Pier, Southsea, and that was from the west, as shown by the Southern Railway paddler *Shanklin* backing all the way out.

THE PIER, VENTNOR.

On the south shore of the Isle of Wight, Ventnor, seen here with the first *Monarch* alongside, was so exposed to any wind from the north-east through to the west that calls here were always hit and miss, except in fine weather.

Chapter 30

Accidents

Given the number of excursion paddle steamers operating around the UK, it is a great credit to their captains and crews that there were very few really serious accidents and, after the loss of the *Princess Alice* (1865–1878) in a collision on the Thames in 1878, none involving large-scale loss of life. They sailed in difficult areas with complex winds and tides, went in and out of so many piers and harbours, and navigated through problematic narrow channels in an age when there were far more ships around than there are now, and without the aid of modern electronic navigational kit.

Of course, there were plenty of other incidents. Bumps alongside piers causing damage were regular. Hitting small dinghies was not unknown. Running aground happened, and sometimes there were more serious accidents, leading to the loss of the steamers themselves.

In her third season, on 27 August 1886, *Bournemouth* ran into thick fog in West Bay while returning from Torquay to Bournemouth and approaching Portland Bill. There are two ways to round the bill to avoid the fearful race, which extends its most turbulent water more than a mile out to sea. Either you should stand well out to seawards of everything, or there is a narrow passage, a cable or so wide, right in close to the cliffs, where the sea can be calm in good weather. Capt. Perrin, on the *Bournemouth*, chose the latter.

He would have been aware that the tide sets quite fiercely in a southerly direction down the western side of Portland for most of the tidal cycle, therefore setting all who wish to use the inshore passage down towards the race. He would doubtless have been trying to keep up a little to the north to counteract this.

Also in 1886, the current lighthouse, almost on the bill itself, had yet to be built, and navigational assistance was provided by two lighthouses a little inland and some way from the bill. Keeping up towards the sound of their foghorns may also have encouraged Capt. Perrin to edge even further to the north and into the jaws of disaster.

Whatever the case, around 6 p.m *Bournemouth* slammed straight into the west side of Portland, just north of the bill. Fortunately it was a flat, calm day, and everyone was rescued without loss of life; however, the ship was firmly stuck, with her hull snapped in two just forward of the machinery.

On the same afternoon, the *Empress,* also returning from Torquay to Bournemouth, chose the inshore passage but approached the bill more gingerly and passed through successfully. The *Victoria,* returning from Torquay to Weymouth, took the outside route, standing well out to seawards of the race and homing in on the foghorn on the Shambles lightship, before altering course to the north for Weymouth.

5717. In the Bay, Swanage.

Princess of Wales (1888–1888) ordered from the Clyde yard of Barclay, Curle & Co. for the Southampton–Cowes ferry service had a very short career. Shiny and new, she set off on 16 June 1888 for speed trials against the measured mile off Skelmorlie, where she encountered the 2,058-ton steamer *San Augustin* (1876–1903, previously *Balmoral Castle*), which was also out on trials following a refit. Some confusion seems to have arisen between the pilots on the two ships, with the result that the liner ran straight through the paddler just abaft the paddle box, slicing her in half. The stern section sank straight away, taking three of the shipyard painters with it. The bow was taken in tow, but did not make it far before it too sank. This unfortunate incident had a silver lining for Barclay, Curle & Co., who were given a repeat order for an identical ship straight away. This was the *Solent Queen* (1889–1948), pictured approaching Swanage Pier in the 1920s with the *Monarch* berthed at the old pier.

On 28 June 1932, the *Premier* was approaching the north entrance to Portland Harbour, inward bound, in the early afternoon on one of her regular cruises from Weymouth, when she unexpectedly encountered the submarine HMS *Rainbow* (1930–1940) outward bound. Although ringing 'full astern', the submarine hit the *Premier* near the bow, gouging out a considerable hole. Passengers were transferred to the submarine and other craft, which came to assist, and the *Premier,* taking on water but not in imminent danger of sinking, returned to Weymouth for repairs.

In 1934, the *Duchess of Devonshire* was running from Exmouth and Torquay with new owners, the South Devon & West Bay Steamship Company, maintaining the routes for which she had been built, including those requiring loading passengers over her bow from the Devon beaches. Unfortunately, 27 August proved to be a difficult day for her.

Low water at nearby Exmouth Dock was at 2.50 p.m., coinciding with the afternoon call at Sidmouth. Some low tides are lower than others. Rarely do they go as low as chart datum. Once in a blue moon are they less than that. The tide this afternoon was predicted to drop 0.04 m below chart datum, so this was an exceptionally low tide.

The press reports speak of a swell and this would have exacerbated the problem. Having half a metre of water under you in a flat calm is one thing. Having half a metre of water under you with a half-metre swell means the ship is bouncing on the bottom. T. W. E. Roche recalled in his book, *A Shipman's Tale*, that the *Duchess* caught on a newly exposed groyne and, as she tried to go astern, a hole was torn in her bottom. She would have floated over the top of that groyne on most low tides.

A tug was summoned and, on the rising tide, the stern was pulled off the beach, but the volume of water coming in was too much for the pumps. Consequently, the ship was secured with the bow onto the shore and the stern held by kedge anchors, while a larger tug and more pumping equipment were summoned.

During the night, the wind was not kind. The anchors dragged and the *Duchess* fell in broadside onto the beach, this time starboard side to. The larger Brixham-based tug *Dencade* (1909–1946) arrived at around 7 a.m. on the rising tide, and an attempt was made to tow the *Duchess* off. However, the temporary patching of the hole was not enough and, continuing to make water, the ship settled back onto another groyne, making another hole – this time under the main dining saloon aft.

With two holes in her bottom and poor weather in the following days making the situation worse all the time, the *Duchess of Devonshire* was declared a constructive total loss and broken up on the beach.

THE SOUTHAMP   STEAMER LEAVING RYDE PIER, ISLE OF WIGHT.   K.6513.

In 18 June 1956, the *Bournemouth Queen,* seen here leaving Ryde, was sailing down Southampton Water past Fawley when she ran down a 14-foot dinghy containing three soldiers, L/Cpl E. C. Morell, and sappers L. P. Tempest and C. H. Butcher, all from the 17 Port Training Regiment at Marchwood. Female passengers were said to have screamed and hidden their eyes prior to the collision, which left the men desperately trying to keep clear of the churning paddle wheels. Capt. Hinch of the *Bournemouth Queen* said, 'I saw the 14-foot dinghy crossing from port to starboard. I ordered the man at the wheel to port his helm to pass under the dinghy's stern but, instead of keeping on his course, the chap steering the dingy put his helm down and tried to get on the other tack. Unfortunately, we did not have time to clear him.' The three men were rescued by a motor launch from the Fawley Refinery and the *Bournemouth Queen* continued on her trip.

On Sunday 30 August 1959, P & A Campbell's *Glen Usk* was late leaving Bristol on a falling tide and was set onto the Horseshoe Bend in the Avon by the fierce outgoing current, where she became stuck soon after 7 p.m. Passengers were disembarked onto the shore in a rather precarious fashion, and there the ship remained aground until the following morning. She floated off on the rising tide at about 4 a.m., was towed to Penarth for inspection and, after minor repairs, returned to service on Wednesday 2 September. Her master that day, Capt. Neville Cottman, subsequently worked as second mate on the Channel Island mail boat *Caesarea* (1960–1986).

Chapter 31

Radar

One of the earliest navigational wonders to harness the power of electricity was radar. Developed during the period 1935–1940 in various countries as a military instrument for detecting ships and aircraft, radar was pioneered in the UK by Sir Robert Watson-Watt. The basic principle is that electromagnetic waves are sent out from the scanner. Those hitting an object are reflected back to the receiver, and this information is then processed to produce a visible image.

After the Second World War, radar began to become more widely available commercially and was acquired for some merchant ships. It was very expensive to buy, and this, coupled with wonderings about its complexity and fears about its reliability, led many companies to place severe restrictions on its use. After all, you wouldn't want to waste such an expensive bit of kit by wearing it out in fine weather, if that meant that, when the fog came in and you needed it, you found that it had blown a valve through overuse. It was therefore not uncommon for the set on the bridge to be kept in a locked box, to which only the captain had a key.

By the time that radar was affordably priced and in very common use, the day of the UK excursion paddle steamer was over. However, there were a few paddlers that were fitted with this technical wonder in their later years, although they mostly belonged to the railway companies and had a use for ferry work as well as excursions.

The first UK paddle steamer ever to be fitted with radar was the Humber ferry *Tattershall Castle*. This was installed in January 1948 and cost £3,000, then a very considerable sum that would approach £100,000 in today's money. The local press reported that, with over a million passengers using the ferries each year, this would enable them to continue in service even in fog. A month later, there was a front page story in the *Hull Daily Mail* saying that, with visibility down to 40 yards, the radar had been used for the first time, enabling the *Tattershall Castle* to sail on while trawlers and other craft had dropped their anchors to await better conditions. As a result of this success, her sisters *Wingfield Castle* and *Lincoln Castle* (pictured) were equipped with radar as well.

In 1950, the Portsmouth–Ryde paddle steamers *Ryde* and the *Sandown* (1934–1967) were given their first radars, the scanners being planted on the top of their specially shortened foremasts. The third Portsmouth paddler, the *Whippingham*, was not so lucky. She remained radar-less for her whole career, the cost of fitting such a device being thought too exorbitant for a ship that ran only on a few peak days each summer.

At the other end of the Solent, the Lymington–Yarmouth diesel-electric paddle vessel *Farringford* acquired radar at some stage between 1950 and 1954.

The earliest excursion paddle steamer not owned by a rich, nationalised railway company to be fitted with radar was P & A Campbell's *Bristol Queen* (pictured at Weymouth in 1963), which had a set put on as part of a promotional deal for her visit to the Coronation Review in the Solent in June 1953. However, it was promptly taken off again afterwards and the *Bristol Queen* remained without this aid to navigation until her last season in 1967, when a set was installed. In 1956, her last season on the south coast, the same company's *Glen Gower* (1922–1960) received a radar for her international trips from Brighton, Eastbourne and Hastings to Boulogne.

On the Clyde, the *Caledonia*, *Waverley*, *Talisman* and *Jeanie Deans* (pictured at Greenock in November 1965) were all fitted with radar in around 1959/60.

Chapter 32

Pier Toll Prosecution

Tolls were charged at most piers around the UK. Sometimes they were included in the steamer fares and sometimes they weren't, in which case intending passengers had to pay an additional charge to the pier on top of their steamer ticket. Inevitably, this annoyed some people, who became even more irritated if they found that their journey involved more than one steamer and more than one pier, with each pier charging a separate toll on the same trip.

For example, after Boscombe Pier opened about a mile east of Bournemouth Pier in 1889, some steamers called at both piers on their trips outward and inward bound, but some didn't. In May 1891, Mr William Simmonds, a gentleman residing in Boscombe, joined the *Brodick Castle* at Boscombe in the morning for a trip to Portsmouth but, on the return in the evening, *Brodick Castle* called only at Bournemouth, transferring her Boscombe passengers onto the *Lord Elgin* for the final leg.

That would have been fine, except that the corporation that owned Bournemouth Pier insisted on charging a pier toll of 1*d* to all who disembarked from the *Brodick Castle* and walked across their pier to join the *Lord Elgin*.

Mr Simmonds refused to cough up, claiming that it was collusion between the corporation and the steamboat operators to extract yet more money from visitors. As a result, he was taken to court, convicted of failing to pay the pier toll and fined 18*s* to include costs. He asked for a receipt, but was refused. They knew how to treat difficult customers in Bournemouth.

Majestic backing out from Boscombe Pier.

Monarch and *Majestic* alongside Bournemouth Pier.

Chapter 33

Fines on the Thames

One of the problems of operating paddle steamers on the Thames was the vast distances that had to be covered in order to get passengers from London to Ramsgate or Clacton and back home again before the buses stopped in the evening. To do this required the steamers to push on at full speed all the way down and back up the river in pretty much all circumstances, and most particularly when punching adverse tides.

Producing wash doesn't matter much at sea but, on a river, it matters a lot, particularly when there are wharfs, jetties and buoys, with ships, barges and lighters alongside loading cargos. Although the steamers did slow down where really necessary, pushing on and keeping to time was a high priority. Six five-minute slowdowns on the way out and six more on the way home would have made them an hour late back. As a result, managements were summoned to court often and claims for wash damage were regular.

Thames Queen (1898–1948, previously *Queen of Southend* and *Yarmouth Belle*) alongside at Ramsgate in 1939.

Chapter 34

Trouble on the *Monarch*

In August 1957, a hotel worker of no fixed address was arrested and remanded in custody, charged with stealing £5 15s 7d from a till in the bar of the *Monarch*. As the steamer was tying up at Bournemouth, the barman had left the bar unattended; the accused was the only customer in it. When he returned, he found that his keys were missing and that money had been taken from the till. The keys were then spotted on deck, close to where the accused was standing, and a search of his pockets revealed some crumpled £1 notes and loose change in his raincoat pocket. The man was detained by the crew and the police were called. Later in court, the defendant said, 'I don't remember the incident, your honour.'

In September 1959, a fifteen-year-old schoolgirl from Manchester recounted to Poole juvenile court that she 'had felt spiteful towards her parents' after her father had accused her of stealing money from her mother's purse. She had run away to see a crew member of a paddle steamer at Poole (the *Monarch*), whom she had met and talked to on a previous family holiday. The girl spent the night aboard with this crew member, who was married and apparently had seven children, because she said that she 'was scared of being on her own and wanted him to stay'.

You can just imagine how a story like this would pan out in today's climate, with, in all likelihood, the crew member being arrested and thrown in the slammer straight away. In 1959, the girl was sent to a remand home for reports.

Monarch in the Weymouth
Backwater in January 1961.

Chapter 35

Torquay Paddler Banned

In 1960, Cdr Edmund Rhodes bought the *Princess Elizabeth* from Red Funnel of Southampton and put her into service, running coastal trips from Torquay to the River Dart, Exmouth and Sidmouth, in addition to landing trips to Lyme Regis and initially to Plymouth.

This did not go down well with the numerous operators of the small motor vessels already running from Torquay. As soon as they knew she was coming, they raised all manner of objections about her safety, her smoke, and any other excuse that they could conjure up to denounce her. The 1960 season passed in a spirit of ill will on all sides, without anyone actually coming to blows, and there was more of the same in 1961 with, if anything, the situation getting worse.

Then her opponents were presented with an opportunity that their lobbying could exploit to their advantage. All the small Torquay boats were licenced by the local council, and their harbourmaster had his own system for assessing when he considered the weather suitable for them to sail. If he thought it was too windy and they shouldn't go out at all, he hoisted a red flag from the pier. If he thought they should sail only within Torbay, he hoisted a blue flag.

The *Princess Elizabeth* had a seagoing Class III certificate issued by the BOT; her captain, Harry Defrates, thought that this flag system did not apply to him and consequently ignored it. He was on sound legal ground here but, politically, this may have been an unwise move.

The local boat owners were incensed and made their angry feelings known to the harbourmaster. He decided to take a stand to enforce the same rule for all, and the council backed him. An impasse ensued, with the gates to Haldon Pier being locked, thus preventing a road tanker from bunkering the ship. This effectively stopped her services.

This story of a rebel steamer against officialdom had legs, and ended up being reported in most of the national press, on radio and television. The council admitted that its red/blue flag system had no legal backing to stop a ship licenced by the BOT, but maintained that nobody could force them to allow a fuel tanker onto their own property, down their own pier, to refuel somebody else's ship.

That was that for the *Princess Elizabeth* at Torquay. She sailed away in mid-September 1961 to lay-up for the winter at Weymouth and never ran from the resort again, although she did make one further call on Sunday 27 June 1965 on a PSPS charter from Weymouth.

Princess Elizabeth alongside Haldon Pier, Torquay, on 27 June 1965.

Another view of *Princess Elizabeth* alongside at Torquay in 1965.

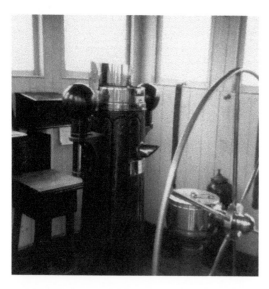

The brass wheel and binnacle in *Princess Elizabeth*'s wheelhouse in 1965.

The flag locker and radio in *Princess Elizabeth*'s wheelhouse. Note the tarpaulin hanging over the radio to protect it from drips from the very leaky deck-head above. The small brass panel to the right of the radio was for emergency contact with the engineer, with buttons for 'stand-by', 'stop', 'ahead' and 'astern'.

Princess Elizabeth's engine-room telegraph at 'Finished with Engines', shortly after her arrival to lay-up in Weymouth in September 1961.

Chapter 36

Mr Jennings Tries and Fails

Freshwater was withdrawn from her Lymington–Yarmouth run in 1959 and bought by Herbert Jennings, who decided to launch his own paddle-steamer preservation project, putting the ship into service sailing on the Sussex coast.

Newly renamed *Sussex Queen,* she was late starting as a number of factors delayed her, including the refit, new requirements imposed by the BOT and crew problems. Mr Jennings recounted in a scrapbook that,

> after great difficulty in getting going after all the overhaul work was carried out, we were delayed for nearly a month in getting the radio with all this time wages going out at the rate of £300 per week plus harbour dues and fuel costs. Another problem was crew. Steam engineers were people of a past age, firemen for a coal fired ship all dead and, when a good one was found, a pig-headed half-Scot upset him so we lost him. Of the deck crew they were generally a scruffy lot of British Rail throw-outs. The mate had little authority. The purser/radio officer was useless and quite unable to look after the tickets or cash. The number of passengers leaving the vessel never tallied with the tickets issued or the money handed in.

At the end of the season, Mr Jennings continued,

> Standing on the end of the pier, I watched my steamer swing and lay a course for Newhaven around Beachy Head. I watched her disappear into the setting sun. To me, it was a sad sight. I felt very lonely as I pondered if this was to be her last trip from Eastbourne. Regrettably it was. Due to the bungling of our affairs by my company's solicitor, we lost our concession with the Palace Pier Company.

Sussex Queen retired to Topsham on the River Exe for the winter, where some wag painted out the 'Sus' of *Sussex* in the name on her bow. For the 1961 season, Mr Jennings recalled,

> Many alternatives were considered, including possible operation in the Bristol Channel jointly with P & A Campbell, but this fell through and I was thrown back onto fighting my way into Bournemouth, where an opening existed owing to Cosens having disposed of their *Monarch*. Fight my way it was, with every obstacle being placed before me. This is a story of most unbelievable intrigue and even sabotage.

Renamed *Swanage Queen*, she sailed from Bournemouth in 1961, running mostly on the Swanage service with one day a week to the Isle of Wight, but the short nine-week season was not a success. Crew problems were once again endemic and a drama developed when the ship nearly sank alongside Poole Quay; Mr Jennings believing that someone had deliberately opened her seacocks.

Swanage Queen was put up for sale and sold for scrap in Belgium in April 1962.

Freshwater alongside at Lymington in 1930 beyond her smaller consort *Solent* (1902–1948, before becoming *Bert's Café* at Porchester).

Sussex Queen berthing at Eastbourne for the first time on 30 June 1960.

Sussex Queen's stern, showing the emergency steering wheel and binnacle aft for use in case of a failure in the main steering system.

A deck view of the *Sussex Queen*, alongside at Eastbourne on 1 July 1960.

Sussex Queen leaving Eastbourne on 9 September 1960 for Brighton and lay-up in Exmouth.

Deck view of *Swanage Queen* outward bound down the Needles Channel, Isle of Wight, on her way back to Bournemouth, Swanage and Poole in 1961.

Herbert Jennings on deck of the *Sussex Queen*, alongside at Newhaven in 1960. For all his difficulties and ultimate lack of success with paddle-steamer preservation, I cannot help but admire Mr Jennings. At a time when paddle steamers were going to the breakers at an ever-increasing rate, he tried to stem that tide. He put his money where his mouth was and worked tirelessly to achieve that goal. Never daunted, he made a subsequent and unsuccessful attempt to buy the *Medway Queen* and spent his later years running a small passenger launch from Exmouth.

Chapter 37

Jeanie Deans Sails South

In August 1965, Don Rose bought the Clyde paddler *Jeanie Deans*. She was moved to Lamont's Shipyard at Port Glasgow for slipping and other necessary work, and a crew was engaged to steam her round to the Medway under the command of Capt. Stanley Woods, who had been master of the *Princess Elizabeth* at Weymouth that summer. I had learnt to steer aboard the *Lizzie* that year in my school holidays and so, knowing of my interest in paddlers, he invited me to come along for the trip. I was only fourteen at the time, but it looked as though this would fit in with the half-term holidays, so my parents said yes and off I went.

Compared with the Weymouth paddle steamers I had known, *Jeanie Deans* was huge, with her two great funnels, enormous triple-expansion engine and a bridge equipped with the modern wonder of radar. Much work had been done to prepare the ship for her new life, but she was in a poor state generally. The decks leaked. There was the accumulation of more than a year's dirt everywhere. The cabins, including the mattresses, were damp. Capt. Woods promptly abandoned any thought of moving into the captain's cabin abaft the wheelhouse and immediately decamped to a hotel ashore at the company's expense, commandeering the purser's office with its steel, and hence watertight, deck-head for his use in due course.

The following morning, *Jeanie Deans* shifted ship from Lamont's jetty into their basin for additional work. The next day, we were ready for trials and, with a pilot aboard as well as Don Rose clutching a plate of smoked-salmon sandwiches, we backed out into the Clyde and proceeded down river.

Jeanie Deans was still capable of a good turn of speed and easily overtook one of the Gourock to Dunoon ferries, but there were lots of things that were not quite right. When the whistle wire was pulled to give a cheery blast, it came away in Capt. Woods's hand. When the fire hydrants were tested, not only did the hose pipes leak but so did some of the steel pipes feeding them. The list of defects was long.

Departure south was scheduled for Friday 5 November, but there was a further delay while the chief engineer was taken to hospital in an ambulance with stomach pains. An engineer was hastily drafted in from Lamont's to take us as far as Stranraer and to train up the second engineer in the mysteries of *Jeanie*'s engine room, and we sailed about teatime.

We sped along into the gathering darkness until, off Dunoon, the paddle beat got slower and a message came up to say that the boiler water feed pump was not working and the boiler was nearly out of water. We dropped the anchor and enjoyed the modest Guy Fawkes fireworks displays on each bank of the Clyde while the engineers fixed the problem.

After an hour or so, the anchor came up and we continued until we were off Pladda, when again the paddle beat got slower and we were forced to stop for more remedial work. Capt. Woods looked rather anxiously at the chart, commented on how deep the water was, even close up to the shore in places, and wondered if there was anywhere near enough chain to drop the anchor out there. Fortunately, the engineers got things going around midnight and we came to anchor off Stranraer to await daylight to go in.

Among the multiplicity of changes that have overtaken us in the last fifty years, one has been the development of radio communications. In 1965, VHF for inter-ship and port radio barely existed and, although seagoing paddlers like the *Jeanie Deans* were equipped with medium-frequency radios, their regular use was discouraged, as the broadcast range was so large that the whole system would have clogged up if too many people had used it at once. The staff at Stranraer were therefore much surprised to find the *Jeanie Deans* steaming up to their jetty unannounced early to take on water the following morning.

There are many ingredients in the fortunes of any venture. The necessary skills, hard work and plenty of cash to dig yourself out of holes are just some, but a measure of good luck is always beneficial in any equation of success. That was something that seemed to be in very short supply for the *Jeanie Deans* then and for her following two seasons when trying to run on the Thames as the *Queen of the South*. The wicked hobgoblin who turns well-meant decisions into black farce seemed to have stationed his malevolent wand permanently round each and every corner.

As it was now Saturday and I had to be back at school on Monday, I had to pay off and catch the train home. The crew meanwhile busied themselves filling every available receptacle with spare boiler-feed water for the onward voyage, 'just in case'. This included the lifeboats, which, being rather dry, were passing it straight out again through their clinker-built boards.

At last *Jeanie Deans* cast off and continued on her way to the Medway, where she arrived on Sunday 14 November to lay up for the winter on the buoys off Chatham Dockyard.

Jeanie Deans in the basin at Lamont's Shipyard, Port Glasgow, in late October 1965.

Jeanie Deans's paddle box alongside at Lamont's Shipyard.

Jeanie Deans's windows boarded up for the voyage south from the Clyde to the Medway.

A view from the top of *Jeanie Deans*'s wheelhouse.

Jeanie Deans's engine-room and docking telegraphs. Her bridge wings around the telegraphs had a raised grating, onto which you had to step up. This had been fitted years before for a short captain.

The captain's view from the bridge of the *Jeanie Deans*.

The mate and second engineer trying to open a sounding pipe fitting on deck to check the level of fuel oil being taken into the bunkers.

The second engineer, tanker driver, mate and AB Alfie le Page from Weymouth in conference on deck, still trying to work out the fuel level. Shortly after this picture was taken, a jet of thick black bunker oil shot out from the gooseneck overflow pipe on the side of the funnel above their heads, catching several of the committee on deck below. This did not improve their tempers.

Chapter 38

The Weymouth Paddle-Steamer War

In 1964, just as overseas travel became a viable option for many, and widespread car ownership opened up opportunities previously only within the province of the better off, Weymouth suddenly found itself with two excursion paddle steamers locked in fierce competition for what was by then a much diminished trade.

After a dreadful season in 1963 on the Sussex coast and the Thames, *Consul* returned to Weymouth in 1964 to revive the Lulworth Cove landing trips. This put her in direct competition with the *Princess Elizabeth*, which had taken over her Weymouth sailings in 1963.

Both ships ran to Lulworth Cove, but only the *Consul* called there to land passengers. On Wednesdays and some Fridays in the peak weeks, *Princess Elizabeth* sailed to Yarmouth on the Isle of Wight, leaving the way clear for the *Consul* on the local trips. For potential passengers to tell them apart, their promotional material described them as the 'Red Funnel Ship' and the 'Ship with the Yellow Funnel' respectively.

As may be imagined, relations between the two operators started in a rather less-than-cordial atmosphere, which continued downwards ever after, with allegations of one thing or another being made by one side and counter-allegations of another thing and something else by the other.

Consul's owners were cock-a-hoop when *Princess Elizabeth* ran out of fuel one day in the Solent and received a reprimand from the BOT. *Princess Elizabeth*'s owners were cock-a-hoop when a BOT surveyor turned up to find that *Consul* was overloaded by sixteen passengers and prosecuted her master, who was fined £10.

Consul lasted until the end of August and gave up, leaving the field open for the last fortnight of the season to the *Lizzie*.

One person who greatly benefited from the Weymouth paddle-steamer war was Bob Wills, a former chief engineer of the *Empress* and *Consul*. At that time, he was running the fifty-passenger launch *Topaz* from a pitch on the Pleasure Pier, which all intending passengers for the two paddle steamers had to pass.

Bob's keen commercial antennae soon picked up the fact that he was often asked by people if they were going the right way for the 'Red Funnel Ship' or the 'Ship with the Yellow Funnel'. Ever eager to improve his own business, Bob decided to paint the diminutive funnel of the *Topaz* half red and half yellow, so that, when asked the question again, he could legitimately say, 'This way, madam'. Bob always said that 1964 was one of the best seasons he ever had with his little *Topey*.

Princess Elizabeth, the 'Red Funnel Ship'.

Consul, the 'Ship with the Yellow Funnel'.

The launch *Topaz* in the foreground, minus the diminutive funnel Bob Wills painted half red and half yellow, with the *Monarch* behind.

Epilogue

Although the heyday of UK excursion paddle steamers is now long gone, it is still possible to have a trip on one if you choose your moment. There are around forty-five paddlers still sailing on rivers and lakes in Europe, with concentrations of seventeen in Switzerland and nine at Dresden. Based at Glasgow, the *Waverley* offers excursions from many piers and harbours around the UK each summer and *Kingswear Castle* runs trips on the River Dart. Two more, *Maid of the Loch* on Loch Lomond and *Medway Queen* at Chatham, are currently being restored.

Acknowledgements

E. C. B. Thornton's *South Coast Pleasure Steamers* opened up the history of this fascinating field to my younger self. A number of other books have also been useful for checking facts, including those by Keith Adams, R. B. Adams, Richard Clammer, W. Paul Clegg & John Styring, Chris Collard, Richard H. Coton, Alun D'Orley, Grahame Farr, Geoffrey Grimshaw, Iain MacArthur, John Mackett and T. W. E. Roche, as well as copies of *Paddle Wheels*, journal of the PSPS. The majority of pictures are from my own and my late father's collection, but I am grateful to Pat Bushell, Stafford Ellerman, Peter Ellis, Geof Hamer, Jill Harvey, John Jones, Peter Lamb, Eric Latcham, Capt. Mike Ledger, Ian MacLeod and Peter Stocker for contributing some pictures, cuttings or suggestions. A lot has also been gleaned from many happy hours spent perusing old newspapers from around the country.

About the author: After learning to steer on the *Princess Elizabeth* as a boy, John Megoran subsequently became general manager of the Paddle Steamer Kingswear Castle Trust and sailed as *Kingswear Castle*'s captain for over thirty years on the Medway, Thames and Dart.